The Influence of Human Capital on Economic Growth

ASSOC. PROF. DR (C) RIYANTO WUJARSO, S.E., Ak., M.M., BKP

Jayakarta College of Economic

Jakarta, Indonesia

ACKNOWLEDGEMENTS

I would like to express my deepest gratitude and appreciation to all those who have contributed to the completion of this book, "The Influence of Human Capital on Economic Growth." Without their support, encouragement, and valuable insights, this endeavor would not have been possible.

First and foremost, I would like to extend my heartfelt gratitude to my chairman, Assoc. Prof Revan Andhitiyara, S.E., M.M., CIERM for their guidance, expertise, and unwavering support throughout the entire process of writing this book. Their valuable feedback and constructive criticism have greatly contributed to shaping the content and improving the overall quality of this work.

I would also like to thank the faculty members and staff of the management program at Jayakarta College of Economic for providing me with a conducive learning environment and valuable resources that have enriched my knowledge and understanding of the subject matter.

I am indebted to my family for their love, patience, and constant encouragement. Their unwavering support and belief in my abilities have been a constant source of motivation throughout this journey.

I am grateful to my friends and colleagues who have provided valuable insights, engaging discussions, and moral support. Their input and discussions have contributed significantly to the development of ideas and the refinement of concepts presented in this book.

Finally, I would like to express my sincere appreciation to all the authors, researchers, and scholars whose works and contributions have served as the foundation and inspiration for this book. Their groundbreaking research and insights have significantly shaped the understanding of the influence of human capital on economic growth.

Once again, I extend my heartfelt thanks to everyone who has contributed directly or indirectly to the completion of this book. Your support and collaboration have been invaluable, and I am truly grateful for your involvement.

Assoc. Prof. DR. (C) Riyanto Wujarso, S.E., Ak., M.M., BKP
Management Program, Jayakarta College of Economic

CONTENTS

ABSTRACT

The primary objective of this research is to conduct a comprehensive analysis of the impact of human capital on regional financial development in West Java Province during the period from 2017 to 2019. To achieve this goal, a quantitative research approach is employed, which allows for a systematic examination of the relationships between variables using mathematical analysis techniques. In order to gather data for the analysis, secondary sources are utilized, specifically relying on the data reports provided by the Badan Pusat Statistik (BPS), the Indonesian Central Bureau of Statistics. These reports offer a wealth of information that is crucial for understanding the dynamics of regional financial development in West Java Province.

The research technique employed in this study is panel regression, specifically utilizing the GLS fixed-effect model approach. Panel regression is a statistical method that allows for the examination of both cross-sectional and time series data, making it particularly suitable for analyzing the relationship between human capital and regional financial development over a specific time period. By employing the GLS fixed-effect model, the study takes into account the individual characteristics of each region in West Java Province, thus providing a more accurate estimation of the impact of human capital on financial growth.

The findings of this study shed light on the crucial role of human capital, with a specific focus on the level of education, in influencing economic growth in West Java Province. The estimation results reveal that the education variable possesses the highest coefficient value among all the variables considered, indicating its significant impact on the region's financial development. This underscores the importance of investing in education and improving the educational infrastructure in order to enhance the quality of the workforce and stimulate economic growth.

It is important to note that the relationship between human capital and financial development is not limited to the education variable alone. Other factors, such as the level of health and the labor force, also contribute to the overall impact on economic growth. However, based on the estimation results, the education variable emerges as the most dominant factor influencing financial development in West Java Province. This suggests that efforts to improve the education level of the workforce should be prioritized in order to enhance productivity and drive economic progress.

In light of the research findings, several recommendations are proposed for the local governments in West Java Province. Firstly, it is advised that there should be a substantial increase in regional expenditure allocations specifically dedicated to the education and health sectors. By allocating more resources to these areas, the quality of education and healthcare can be improved, leading to a better-equipped and healthier workforce. This, in turn, can significantly enhance productivity levels, which are crucial for driving financial growth in the region.

Moreover, the findings of this study emphasize the need for a holistic approach to human capital development. Apart from investing in education and health, it is essential to promote skill development programs, vocational training, and continuous learning opportunities for the workforce. This will ensure that individuals are equipped with the necessary skills and competencies to adapt to changing economic demands and contribute effectively to the region's financial development.

This research has provided valuable insights into the impact of human capital on regional financial development in West Java Province. The findings highlight the significant role of education in fostering economic growth and underscore the need for increased investments in education and health sectors. By prioritizing human capital development and creating an enabling environment for skills enhancement, West Java Province can pave the way for sustainable and inclusive financial growth.

I. INTRODUCTION

Development is a multifaceted and intricate process that encompasses a wide array of aspects, including societal transformations, shifts in attitudes, and institutional changes occurring at the national level. It represents progress and advancement in various dimensions, such as economic growth, reduction of income inequality, and the alleviation of poverty (Amann et al., 2006). To achieve successful development, several crucial factors must be fulfilled as they act as key drivers of economic progress. These key drivers can be categorized into two main areas: economic and social metrics, both of which play integral roles in the development process.

One commonly used economic indicator to evaluate the success of an economy is the rate of economic growth (Camacho, 2015). Economic growth serves as a reliable predictor when assessing the outcomes of economic changes introduced by a country or region (Umiyati, 2014). It is measured by comparing the output of goods and services from one year to another. An increase in the output signifies economic growth, demonstrating how economic development can generate higher revenue and improve social welfare within a specific timeframe. A surge in economic growth for a country or region indicates a thriving economy, suggesting progress and prosperity (Putri, 2015).

In addition to economic factors, social metrics also play a significant role in the development process. Social indicators encompass various aspects of well-being, including education, healthcare, and living standards. These metrics reflect the overall quality of life and societal progress within a country or region. Improvements in education, for instance, contribute to the overall development of human capital, fostering innovation, productivity, and economic growth. Access to quality healthcare services and a secure social welfare system are essential for ensuring the well-being and inclusivity of all members of society.

The interplay between economic and social metrics is vital in achieving holistic development. While economic growth is crucial for generating wealth and improving material conditions, it is equally important to ensure that the benefits of development are distributed equitably and reach all segments of society. Addressing income inequality and poverty alleviation are central aspects of inclusive development. By implementing policies that promote equal opportunities, social protection, and sustainable development practices, nations can strive towards balanced and comprehensive progress.

Development is a multifaceted process that encompasses societal transformations, shifts in attitudes, and institutional changes at the national level. It involves various dimensions, including economic growth, reduction of income inequality, and the alleviation of poverty. Economic and social metrics serve as key drivers of development, with economic growth being a commonly used indicator to assess the success of an economy. Social metrics, such as education and healthcare, contribute to the overall well-being and inclusivity of society. Achieving holistic development requires addressing both economic and social aspects, ensuring equitable distribution of benefits and promoting sustainable practices.

Human capital, a term encompassing various meanings, refers to the knowledge, expertise, competence, and other characteristics possessed by individuals that are relevant to economic activities (Becker, 2009). It goes beyond mere labor and should be treated as a production factor on par with physical capital. Adam Smith, a prominent economist, recognized that humans are the primary determinant of a nation's prosperity. Even natural resources hold little value without resourceful individuals to effectively cultivate them. In essence, human capital is the key to economic growth, as physical wealth loses its worth without high-quality human capital (Spengler, 1977).

Capital, in general, refers to the intangible assets represented by the knowledge and skills possessed by individuals. Human capital is acquired through education or training and contributes to the production of goods and services. Kumar (2006) identifies four dimensions of human capital that impact economic development :

First and foremost, "human resources" output quality is a critical input variable in economic operations. The term "human resources" refers to the people who provide their labor, expertise, and skills to an economy's production and development processes. The term "output feature" in this context refers to the tangible and intangible results produced by human resources as a result of their involvement in economic activities. The output characteristic of human resources includes a variety of elements that support societal advancement and economic prosperity. The workforce's productivity is one of the important factors. Productivity levels are determined by things like education, training, experience, and talents that people have. An educated and highly competent labor often displays better levels of productivity, which in turn increases production and efficiency in economic activity.

However, the output characteristic of human resources goes beyond productivity to encompass creativity and breakthroughs in technology. New ideas, the creation and adoption of new technology, and industry innovation are all capabilities of human resources. These inventions may lead to enhanced manufacturing procedures, the creation of fresh goods and services, and general economic advancement.

The output characteristic of human resources also includes the caliber of the products and services provided. The caliber of goods and services offered to customers is directly influenced by the workforce's abilities and knowledge. The likelihood that a workforce will manufacture high-quality goods and provide excellent services increases with education and training, which can boost industry competitiveness and support economic growth.

It is important to note that the output feature of human resources is not solely determined by the quantity of individuals available in the labor market but also by their quality. While population size is a contributing factor to economic growth, it is the skills, knowledge, and capabilities of the workforce that ultimately determine the output and impact on the economy. Therefore, investing in human capital development through education, training, and skill enhancement programs is crucial for maximizing the output feature of human resources.

Secondly, the accumulation of human resources generates favorable externalities that have a profound impact on productivity, ultimately leading to endogenous development. The term "endogenous development" refers to the process of sustainable economic growth and progress that originates from within an economy, driven by its internal factors rather than external influences.

The accumulation of human resources refers to the increase in the quantity and quality of the workforce over time. This can be achieved through various means, such as investments in education, training programs, skill development initiatives, and health promotion. As the quantity and quality of human resources increase, positive externalities begin to emerge, creating a ripple effect that influences the overall productivity and development of an economy.

One of the key externalities generated by the accumulation of human resources is knowledge spillover. When individuals acquire new skills, knowledge, and expertise, they not only apply them to their own work but also share them with their colleagues and peers. This sharing of knowledge leads to an increase in the collective knowledge base of the workforce and facilitates innovation and technological advancements. As a result, productivity levels rise, leading to improved economic performance.

Moreover, the accumulation of human resources fosters a culture of learning and continuous improvement within an economy. As individuals acquire new knowledge and skills, they become more adaptable and responsive to changing market conditions. This adaptability translates into increased efficiency and effectiveness in various economic activities. Additionally, a well-educated and skilled workforce is better equipped to embrace new technologies and adopt innovative practices, further enhancing productivity and competitiveness.

Also, the development of social capital is aided by the accumulation of human resources. The networks, ties, and trust formed by people and organizations within a society are referred to as social capital. People form social networks that enable cooperation, information exchange, and resource mobilization when human resources are amassed via investments in education and training. The collaboration and coordination between many stakeholders is improved by these social networks, which results in more efficient and effective economic activity.

A positive cycle of development is produced by the positive externalities brought about by the buildup of human resources. Productivity gains make the economy more competitive, luring investments and promoting economic expansion. As a result of this increase, more funds are allotted for the development of human capital, which boosts productivity and keeps the endogenous development cycle going.

It is important to note that the accumulation of human resources and the resulting externalities are not isolated phenomena. They are closely intertwined with other factors such as institutional frameworks, infrastructure development, and supportive policies. These factors create an enabling environment that facilitates the accumulation and utilization of human resources, amplifying the positive impact on productivity and endogenous development.

The accumulation of human resources generates favorable externalities that enhance productivity and contribute to endogenous development. Knowledge spillover, a culture of learning, and the formation of social capital are some of the key externalities that arise from investments in human capital. These externalities create a virtuous cycle of development, where increased productivity leads to economic growth, which, in turn, fuels further investments in human capital. By recognizing the importance of human resources and fostering their accumulation, economies can unlock their full potential and achieve sustainable development.

Thirdly, the accumulation of intellectual resources fosters increased creativity and research and development (R&D), leading to endogenous growth. Intellectual resources refer to the knowledge, skills, and expertise possessed by individuals and organizations that contribute to innovation, problem-solving, and the generation of new ideas and technologies.

When an economy invests in the accumulation of intellectual resources, it creates an environment that encourages and supports creativity and innovation. Individuals with higher levels of education and specialized knowledge are more likely to engage in entrepreneurial activities, develop new products and services, and introduce technological advancements. This entrepreneurial spirit and innovation-driven mindset are crucial for achieving endogenous growth.

Increased research and development (R&D) activities are one way that the accumulation of intellectual resources encourages creativity and innovation. Research and development (R&D) is the methodical, scientific pursuit of new knowledge, novel applications of existing knowledge, and the creation of novel goods and technology. R&D expenditures contribute to expanding the frontiers of knowledge and advancing technology, which in turn promotes economic growth.

Economies may foster a culture that supports experimentation, exploration, and the search for novel ideas by committing money to R&D. New technologies, procedures, and goods are created as a result, enhancing production, efficiency, and competitiveness. For instance, greater R&D spending in fields like biotechnology, computer technology, and renewable energy may result in ground-breaking inventions that spur economic expansion and birth new businesses.

And also, human capital plays a crucial role in driving production and promoting social and individual growth. It encompasses the knowledge, expertise, and characteristics possessed by individuals, which contribute to economic activities. The accumulation of human capital leads to favorable externalities and increased creativity, ultimately fostering endogenous development and economic growth. Therefore, recognizing the significance of human capital and investing in its development are crucial for nations to thrive in the competitive global economy.

The impact of human capital on the economy extends beyond production and product development. Fleisher et al. (2010) found that human capital has a positive influence on production and product development in cross-province studies. It is widely acknowledged as a crucial factor determining competitiveness and economic development. However, recent data on employment and growth in the European Union (EU) have revealed some shortcomings in this conventional perspective. Simply possessing human capital does not guarantee economic prosperity on its own (Hanushek, 2013).

The focus of this research is to examine the extent of human capital's influence on the economy of West Java Province. West Java was selected as the focal point of the study due to its superior economic growth compared to several other regions during specific years. Additionally, its proximity to Jakarta, the capital city and financial center of Indonesia, adds significance to its analysis. The aim is to understand how the accumulation of human capital in West Java contributes to its economic growth and development. By studying the region's educational attainment levels, skill development initiatives, and workforce characteristics, we can gain insights into the role of human capital in shaping the economy.

The research will employ a comprehensive methodology, including data collection, statistical analysis, and economic modeling, to examine the relationship between human capital and economic growth in West Java. It will consider various indicators such as educational attainment, skills training, and employment patterns to assess the quality and quantity of human capital in the region. The findings will provide valuable insights for policymakers, businesses, and educational institutions to make informed decisions regarding investments in human capital development.

To summarize, human capital holds immense importance in driving production and fostering economic growth. Its accumulation leads to favorable externalities, increased creativity, and enhanced productivity. However, the mere presence of human capital does not guarantee economic prosperity; it requires effective utilization and integration with other factors. The research on the influence of human capital on the economy of West Java Province will shed light on the specific dynamics of this region and contribute to the broader understanding of the role of human capital in economic development.

1.1 Literature Review

Becker, G. S. (2009). "Human Capital: A Theoretical and Empirical Analysis, with Special Reference to Education."

Gary S. Becker's fundamental book, "Human Capital: A Theoretical and Empirical Study, with Particular Reference to Education," examines the economics of education and the idea of "human capital." In order to study the link between education, wages, and the building up of human capital over the course of a lifetime, Becker's analysis blends theory and actual results. The necessity of investing in one's human capital through education and training is emphasized in the book, which also underlines the influence that families have on a person's human capital. Moreover, it covers the effects of on-the-job training as well as the connection between pay and marginal product. The importance of human capital in economic growth and development is emphasized in the book's conclusion.

Although Becker's book offers a thorough examination of the economics of human capital, it would benefit from a more in-depth examination of the social and cultural aspects that affect the development of human capital. Despite the fact that the book's primary focus is on the economic advantages of education and training, it falls short in its attempt to adequately address the wider societal consequences of human capital. The investigation might have gone further into the impact that government policies play in encouraging investments in human capital and resolving disparities in access to education and training. Also, the book might have discussed how gender, race, and socioeconomic status affect the development of human capital because they have a big influence on educational possibilities and results.

And also, the book's emphasis on the economic benefits of human capital overlooks the intrinsic value of education and the development of individuals as well-rounded citizens. Education is not solely a means to increase earnings, but also a pathway to personal growth, critical thinking, and social mobility. By solely focusing on the economic returns of education, the book neglects the broader societal benefits that education brings, such as fostering social cohesion, promoting democratic values, and reducing inequality.

Another limitation of the book is its narrow focus on formal education and on-the-job training. While these are important components of human capital, the book could have explored other forms of human capital investment, such as informal learning, skills acquired through hobbies or community engagement, and the development of social and emotional intelligence. These aspects of human capital are often overlooked but can have significant impacts on individuals' personal and professional lives.

Hanushek, E. A. (2013). "Economic Growth in Developing Countries: The Role of Human Capital."

The article discusses the role of improved schooling in developing countries and the controversy surrounding whether increased school attainment guarantees improved economic conditions. It argues that cognitive skills, rather than just school attainment, are strongly related to individual earnings and economic growth. The article emphasizes the need to shift the focus to school quality, as developing countries have larger skill deficits compared to developed countries. It also highlights the importance of better measures of human capital and explores the impact of different measures on long-run growth models. The article concludes by discussing the progress and challenges of improving school attainment in developing countries and the need for major structural changes in schooling institutions.

While the article provides valuable insights into the relationship between schooling, cognitive skills, and economic growth in developing countries, there are a few areas that could be further explored. Firstly, the article focuses primarily on cognitive skills as a measure of human capital, but it does not delve into the potential implications of other factors, such as health and nutrition, on human capital development. Further research could investigate the impact of these factors on economic growth and development in developing countries.

Second, the essay contends that higher education levels have no appreciable influence on economic expansion. It does not, however, offer a comprehensive study of the possible causes for this lack of impact. Future studies might look into the exact elements that contribute to postsecondary education's modest impact on economic growth and see whether there are any circumstances or scenarios under which it might have a more substantial impact.

Lastly, while the paper emphasizes the significance of raising school quality, it offers no concrete suggestions or methods for doing so. Future studies might concentrate on discovering efficient programs and initiatives that can raise the standard of education in underdeveloped nations, especially in terms of fostering cognitive development and resolving skill deficiencies.

The essay also briefly discusses the trade-off between vocational and general education as well as the possible drawbacks of vocational education in terms of technological adaptation. It does not, however, offer a thorough study of this trade-off and its effects on economic growth in emerging nations. Additional research on this subject may provide insight into the ideal ratio of general and vocational education, as well as how it affects both short- and long-term employability and adaptability.

II. Method

The book titled "The Influence of Human Capital on Economic Growth" employs a range of research methods to explore the relationship between human capital and economic growth.

This book utilizes various methods, including:

1. Quantitative Research Methodology.

This study utilizes a quantitative research methodology, which involves the analysis of data using mathematical techniques. Quantitative analysis aims to test hypotheses by quantifying variables and interpreting the results using statistical procedures. This approach provides a systematic and objective way to examine the relationship between variables.

2. Data Sources.

The Central Statistical Agency is one of the secondary sources used to get the data for this study (BPS). Secondary data is information that is gathered from other written or spoken sources but is indirectly derived from the study object. The secondary data from the BPS is a trustworthy and complete source of information about the variables of relevance in the context of this study.

A prominent government agency in Indonesia that is in charge of gathering, examining, and distributing statistical data is the Central Statistical Agency (BPS). It compiles information from a range of sources, including surveys, censuses, administrative records, and other pertinent sources. The study's utilization of secondary data from the BPS guarantees the accuracy and consistency of the data.

The data used in this study covers the period from 2017 to 2019, providing a sufficient time frame to analyze the relationship between human capital and economic growth. By examining data from multiple years, the study can capture trends and changes over time, allowing for a more comprehensive analysis.

The study's primary focus is on 25 metropolitan areas in West Java. With this choice, the connection between human capital and economic development in a particular area may be locally analyzed. The study can take into consideration regional differences and certain contextual elements that may have an impact on the connection under examination by limiting its geographic reach. Overall, using secondary data from the Central Statistical Agency (BPS) gives the study a solid and trustworthy base. A thorough investigation of the link between human capital and economic growth in a specific local context is possible because of the data's extensive temporal coverage and emphasis on particular metropolitan districts in West Java.

3. Variables and Hypotheses.

The study focuses on operationalizing and examining the relationship between several key variables and economic growth. The dependent variable in this study is economic growth, which serves as the primary outcome of interest. Economic growth refers to the increase in a country's production of goods and services over a specific period, often measured by indicators such as Gross Domestic Product (GDP). The study identifies three independent variables that are believed to have a significant influence on economic growth.

These independent variables are:

- Level of education

This variable captures the educational attainment and quality of the workforce in a particular region or country. It considers factors such as literacy rates, enrollment in formal education systems, and the availability of skilled labor. Education is considered an important driver of economic growth as it enhances productivity, fosters innovation, and improves overall human capital.

- Level of health

This variable focuses on the health status and well-being of the population. It takes into account indicators such as life expectancy, healthcare accessibility, and disease prevalence. Healthy individuals are more likely to participate actively in the labor force, leading to increased productivity and economic growth. Additionally, a healthier population reduces healthcare costs and promotes a more efficient allocation of resources.

- Workforce

This variable represents the quantity and quality of the labor force available for production activities. It encompasses factors such as employment rates, labor force participation, and skills levels. A skilled and productive workforce is crucial for economic growth, as it drives innovation, improves efficiency, and attracts investment.

Based on the importance of these variables and their potential impact on economic development, the study formulates hypotheses regarding their relationships with economic growth. These hypotheses are tentative statements that propose the expected direction and strength of the relationships between the independent variables (education, health, workforce) and the dependent variable (economic growth). The hypotheses provide a framework for testing and analyzing the empirical data collected in the study.

By examining and analyzing these variables and their hypothesized relationships, the study aims to contribute to the understanding of the factors that drive economic growth. It seeks to provide empirical evidence regarding the significance of education, health, and the workforce in promoting sustainable economic development. The findings from this analysis can inform policymakers and stakeholders in designing effective strategies and policies to enhance economic growth by investing in human capital development.

4. Panel Regression Analysis.

In this study, panel regression analysis is employed as a method to analyze the data. Panel regression is a statistical technique that is particularly suitable for studying data that involves multiple individuals or entities observed over a period of time. It allows for the examination of both individual-specific and time-specific effects, providing a comprehensive analysis of the data.

The panel regression model used in this study is the GLS fixed-effect model. The GLS (Generalized Least Squares) estimation method is utilized to account for the presence of heteroscedasticity and autocorrelation in the data. By incorporating fixed effects, the model controls for individual heterogeneity, capturing unobserved characteristics that may vary across entities but remain constant over time. This helps in mitigating the potential bias that may arise from unobserved variables affecting the relationships between the variables of interest.

The advantage of using the GLS fixed-effect model is that it allows for more accurate estimation of the relationships between the variables under investigation. By controlling for individual heterogeneity, the model provides a clearer understanding of the specific effects of the independent variables on the dependent variable, while taking into account the uniqueness of each entity in the panel data. Panel regression analysis using the GLS fixed-effect model in this study enhances the validity and reliability of the findings. It enables a rigorous examination of the relationships between the variables of interest, while considering both individual-specific and time-specific effects. This approach contributes to a comprehensive understanding of the research questions and helps to generate more precise estimates of the effects of human capital on economic growth. In order to analyze the link between economic growth and factors like education level, health level, and workforce, this study employs a quantitative research methodology and makes use of secondary data from the Central Statistical Agency (BPS). Panel regression with the GLS fixed-effect model, which offers a thorough investigation of the research questions and hypotheses, is the analytic method of choice.

This study utilizes a quantitative research methodology, which involves the analysis of data using mathematical techniques. Quantitative analysis, as defined by Sugiyono (2011), aims to test hypotheses by quantifying variables and interpreting the results using statistical procedures. Similarly, Martono (2010) describes the quantitative approach as a research method that involves collecting and expressing data in numerical form, while maintaining a standardized and objective distance between the researcher and the object of study through the use of measuring instruments.

In this study, the data is obtained from secondary sources, which refers to information indirectly derived from the research object but obtained from other written or oral sources. Specifically, the data is sourced from the Central Statistics Agency (BPS) and covers the period from 2017 to 2019. The focus of the study is on 25 urban districts within West Java.

To operationalize the variables, this research considers economic growth as the dependent variable. The independent variables include the level of education, level of health, and the workforce. These variables are essential factors to investigate as they are believed to have an impact on economic development. The chosen analysis technique for this study is panel regression, specifically using the GLS fixed-effect model. Panel regression is a suitable approach as it accounts for both individual and time-specific effects, allowing for a comprehensive analysis of the data.

In summary, this study adopts a quantitative research method characterized by the utilization of mathematical analysis techniques. The data used is secondary data obtained from the Central Statistics Agency (BPS) and covers 25 urban districts in West Java from 2017 to 2019. The research aims to examine the relationship between economic growth (dependent variable) and independent variables such as education level, health level, and workforce. The chosen analysis technique is panel regression with the GLS fixed-effect model, which allows for a robust examination of the research questions and hypotheses.

III. RESULT & DISCUSSION

The findings from the panel regression model, which incorporates economic growth as the dependent variable and education level, health level, and labor force as independent variables, are illustrated in Table 1 provided below.

Variable	Coefficient	Std. Error	t-statistics	Prob.
Constant (C)	-4.475710	0.810260	-5.535600	0.0000
Education (RLS)	0.913128	0.152346	6.051285	0.0001
Health (AHH)	0.754085	0.198896	3.873943	0.0001
Workforce (AK Diploma/S1)	0.332211	0.036349	9.137963	0.0000
Adjusted R-squared	0.783026			
F-statistic	17.33327			
Prob. (F-statistic)	0.000000			

Table 1

Here's a detailed explanation of each column in the table :

➔ **Variable**

This column lists the variables included in the regression analysis. In this case, the variables are "Constant (C)," "Education (RLS)," "Health (AHH)," and "Workforce (AK Diploma/S1)." These variables represent different factors related to human capital.

➔ **Coefficient**

The coefficient column represents the estimated coefficients for each variable. These coefficients indicate the expected change in the dependent variable (economic growth) for a one-unit change in the corresponding independent variable, holding other variables constant. For example, a one-unit increase in the "Education (RLS)" variable is associated with an estimated increase of 0.913128 units in economic growth.

→ Std. Error

The standard error column shows the standard errors associated with the estimated coefficients. The standard error represents the average amount by which the estimated coefficients might vary from the true population value. Smaller standard errors indicate greater precision in the coefficient estimates.

→ t-statistics

The t-statistics column displays the calculated t-values for each coefficient. The t-value measures the significance of each coefficient by comparing it to its standard error. Higher t-values indicate greater evidence against the null hypothesis (i.e., the coefficient is equal to zero). In general, t-values greater than 2 (in absolute value) are considered statistically significant.

→ Prob.

The probability column represents the p-values associated with the t-statistics. The p-value indicates the probability of obtaining a t-value as extreme as or more extreme than the one observed, assuming the null hypothesis is true. Lower p-values (typically below 0.05) suggest strong evidence against the null hypothesis and indicate statistical significance.

→ Adjusted R-squared

The adjusted R-squared is a measure of how well the independent variables (education, health, and workforce) explain the variation in the dependent variable (economic growth), adjusted for the number of variables and sample size. It ranges from 0 to 1, where higher values indicate a better fit of the regression model to the data.

➜ **F-statistic**

The F-statistic assesses the overall significance of the regression model. It tests the null hypothesis that all the coefficients in the model are equal to zero. Higher F-statistics suggest a better overall fit of the model.

➜ **Prob. (F-statistic)**

The probability associated with the F-statistic represents the p-value for testing the overall significance of the regression model. A low p-value (typically below 0.05) indicates that the regression model is statistically significant in explaining the variation in the dependent variable.

These statistical values help interpret the significance and reliability of the coefficients and provide insights into the relationships between human capital variables and economic growth in the study.

The findings from the panel regression analysis indicate that the Economic Growth Rate serves as the dependent variable, whereas the independent variables consist of Education, Health, and Labor Force. Based on the preliminary examination, the regression model can be formulated as follows :

$$Y = -4.476 + 0.913\ RLS_{it} + 0.754\ AHH_{it} + 0.332\ AKdiploma/S1_{it} + u$$

The findings obtained from the regression equation shed light on the significant influence of various variables on the Economic Growth Rate.

- The analysis reveals that the Education variable plays a crucial role in driving economic growth, as evidenced by its positive coefficient of 0.913. This indicates that for every one-unit increase in education, there is a corresponding 0.913 percent increase in the economic growth rate.

- The positive coefficient of the Health variable, which stands at 0.754, further emphasizes the importance of health in fostering economic development. A one-unit increase in health is associated with a 0.754 percent increase in economic growth.

- The Labor Force variable exhibits a positive coefficient of 0.332, underscoring the significant contribution of a larger workforce to economic growth. A one-unit increase in the labor force corresponds to a 0.332 percent increase in the economic growth rate.

- The determination coefficient (R2) is a measure of how well the regression model explains the variability in the dependent variable. In this analysis, the adjusted R Square value is used to assess the model's performance, which is 0.783 or 78.3%. This indicates that 78.3% of the contribution to economic growth can be attributed to the education, health, and workforce variables, along with the fixed impact of individual cities. The remaining 21.7% of the contribution to economic growth is influenced by other variables that were not included in the regression equation.

- To examine the hypothesis regarding the impact of the independent variable (Xparallel) on the dependent variable Y (Economic Growth Rate), the F statistical test is employed. The results reveal a calculated F value of 17.333, with a significance level of 0.000. Comparing this estimated F value with the critical F value from the table (2.653), denoted as Sig F (0.000), we find that the estimated F value is statistically significant. However, it is still lower than 5% (0.050), which is the conventional threshold for statistical significance.

These results lead us to the conclusion that H_1, which contends that the variables Health, Education, and Labor Force are Significantly Associated with Economic Growth Rate, is Accepted. H_0, on the other hand, which denotes no appreciable impact, is disregarded. This suggests that a major portion of the variation in the

Economic Growth Rate may be attributed to the interactions between the variables of Education, Health, and Labor Force.
It is significant to note that the model does not account for all of the variation in the Economic Growth Rate, since there are additional factors that are responsible for the remaining 21.7% of the variance that are not accounted for by the regression equation. Consequently, future study should think about including more variables to increase the model's capacity for explanation and give

The t statistical test is a powerful tool used to examine the impact of independent variables on the dependent variable. In this study, the t-test was employed to assess the influence of the independent variable Xpartial on the dependent variable, Economic Growth Rate. The results obtained from Table 1 shed light on the effects of various independent variables on the dependent variable.

These findings demonstrate the multifaceted nature of economic growth, as it is influenced by multiple factors. Education, health, and labor force variables are identified as key determinants in promoting economic development. The positive coefficients of these variables highlight their beneficial impact on the overall economic growth rate. The results underscore the importance of investing in education and health initiatives to enhance human capital and foster a productive workforce.

Additionally, policies aimed at promoting labor force participation can contribute to sustained economic growth. Understanding the specific contributions of these variables provides valuable insights for policymakers and stakeholders in formulating strategies to achieve robust and sustainable economic development.

Firstly, the Education variable exhibited a t count of 6.051, which surpassed the critical t value of 1.973 at a 5 percent margin of error. This indicates a significant positive impact of the Education variable on the economic growth rate. With a significance value of 0.001, lower than the 5 percent alpha level, the Education variable's effect on economic growth is considered highly substantial. These findings highlight the importance of education in driving economic development. A well-educated workforce tends to possess the necessary skills and knowledge to contribute effectively to the growth of the economy.

The Health variable demonstrated a t-value of 3.873, exceeding the critical t value of 1.973. With a significance value of 0.001, the Health variable's impact on the economic growth rate is also deemed significant.

This suggests that improvements in the health sector can have a positive effect on economic growth. When the population enjoys good health and access to quality healthcare services, productivity increases, leading to overall economic advancement.

Moreover, the Labor Force variable exhibited a substantial t value of 9.137, coupled with a significance value of 0.000, which is lower than the 5 percent alpha level. This indicates that the Labor Force variable has a highly significant and positive influence on the economic growth rate. A skilled and productive labor force is a crucial driver of economic development. By investing in workforce development, including training programs and skills enhancement initiatives, regions can create a strong labor force that contributes to economic growth and competitiveness.

To summarize, the statistical analysis conducted in this study confirms that the Education, Health, and Labor Force variables have significant positive effects on the Economic Growth Rate variable. The findings provide robust evidence supporting the acceptance of H_1 and the rejection of H_0, indicating the importance of these factors in driving economic growth. The study emphasizes the need for policymakers and governments to prioritize investments in education, health, and labor force development to foster sustainable economic progress and prosperity.

3.1 Relationship between Education Level and Economic Growth

Education is widely recognized as a fundamental investment in human resources, alongside physical capital investment. It plays a crucial role in enhancing knowledge and improving job skills, which ultimately leads to increased work productivity. The significance of education in driving economic development is highlighted by the calculation findings of this study. The results indicate a significant and positive impact of education on economic growth, with a significance value of 0.001, which is smaller than the alpha of 5 percent or 0.05. These consistent results further reinforce the study's findings.

The analysis presented here aligns with the research conducted by Asiedu (2014), which emphasizes the vital and positive role of education in promoting economic growth. According to Asiedu, increasing education levels can enhance capabilities and serve as a crucial means of developing "human capital" for the future. By investing in education and improving educational opportunities, productivity and income levels can be elevated, both in the present and in the future.

Moreover, the findings of this study support the empirical results of a previous research conducted by Dwi Atmanti (2005). Atmanti's study found that increased investment in human capital through education directly enhances labor productivity. It was observed that an increase in aggregate output is indicative of improved productivity. These findings strongly support the theory of endogenous growth, which underscores the government's role in enhancing human capital and boosting productivity as the driving force behind economic growth.

Education not only provides individuals with the necessary knowledge and skills to perform their jobs effectively but also has broader societal benefits. A well-educated workforce is better equipped to adapt to changes in the economy, technological advancements, and global trends. Education empowers individuals, enabling them to participate actively in economic activities and contribute to innovation and productivity gains.

Also, education plays a crucial role in reducing income inequality and fostering social mobility. By providing equal educational opportunities to all individuals, regardless of their socio-economic background, society can break the cycle of poverty and create a more inclusive and equitable economy. Education acts as a catalyst for social and economic development, empowering individuals and communities to improve their living standards and quality of life.

In the context of West Java Province, investing in education is of paramount importance. As one of the most populous provinces in Indonesia, West Java possesses immense human capital potential. By focusing on improving the quality of education, expanding access to educational institutions, and providing relevant and skill-based training programs, the provincial government can harness this human capital and drive economic growth.

The conclusions of this study imply that local governments in West Java Province should give the education sector higher regional spending priority. They may raise the standard of the labor force, boost job skills, and promote innovation and entrepreneurship by investing greater resources into education. Investments in the health sector should also be taken into account since a population that is educated and in good health is crucial for long-term economic growth.

This study shows the importance of education and its beneficial effects on the financial growth of the West Java Province. Education is a major human capital investment that contributes significantly to economic success. Through raising educational standards, people and communities may realize their full potential, boost output, lessen economic disparity, and promote social mobility. The results highlight the significance of giving education and health investments top priority if West Java Province is to improve the quality of the workforce, increase economic results, and build a wealthy and inclusive society.

3.2 Relationship between Health Level and Economic Growth

The relationship between the level of health and economic growth is a critical factor that shapes the development trajectory of nations. Health is a fundamental aspect of human well-being, and its impact extends beyond individual welfare to the overall quality of human capital. When concerted efforts are made to improve the health sector, it yields positive outcomes for the workforce, ultimately leading to increased productivity and economic advancement.

A substantial body of research has consistently demonstrated the direct and positive influence of health on economic growth. For instance, Handayaniet et al. (2016) conducted a panel analysis that delved into the relationship between health and economic growth. Their findings align with existing literature, further substantiating the understanding that health significantly influences economic development, as measured by indicators such as life expectancy.

The calculations performed in their study revealed a noteworthy insight: a one-year increase in life expectancy corresponds to a remarkable 4 percent increase in productivity. This statistic highlights the tangible impact of health improvements on labor productivity. It reinforces the notion that health can be seen as a form of human capital, emphasizing the value of investing in health-related interventions and policies.

By recognizing the intrinsic connection between health and economic growth, policymakers and stakeholders can shape strategies that promote both individual well-being and national prosperity. Prioritizing health as a crucial determinant of economic growth is essential. By doing so, policymakers can foster a healthier population, which, in turn, enhances the overall quality of life. A healthier population is not only more productive but also less burdened by preventable illnesses, enabling individuals to actively participate in economic activities and contribute to the nation's progress.

Investments in healthcare infrastructure, disease prevention programs, and accessible healthcare services play a vital role in improving health outcomes. By ensuring that individuals have access to quality healthcare, governments can enhance productivity, reduce absenteeism, and lower healthcare costs in the long run. Moreover, prioritizing public health initiatives, such as health education campaigns, sanitation programs, and clean water supply, can significantly improve overall health indicators and promote economic growth.

The benefits of a healthy population extend beyond the individual level. A robust healthcare system and improved health outcomes attract domestic and foreign investments, as businesses value a healthy and productive workforce. Additionally, a healthier population reduces the strain on public resources, such as healthcare expenditure and social welfare programs, allowing governments to allocate resources more efficiently towards other developmental endeavors.

Furthermore, focusing on health as a critical driver of economic growth contributes to long-term sustainability. By investing in preventive measures and promoting a healthy lifestyle, nations can reduce the burden of chronic diseases and improve the overall health profile of their population. This, in turn, translates into lower healthcare costs, increased life expectancy, and improved productivity, creating a positive feedback loop that supports continued economic progress.

The relationship between health and economic growth is undeniable. Health serves as a foundational component of human capital and significantly influences productivity and overall economic development. Prioritizing health interventions and policies is crucial for fostering a healthier population, improving individual well-being, and driving sustained economic progress. By recognizing the importance of health in the development agenda, policymakers can design comprehensive strategies that yield both social and economic benefits, ultimately leading to prosperous and sustainable societies.

3.3 The Relationship of the Labor Force to Economic Growth

In the field of economics, the relationship between population growth, workforce expansion, and economic development has been a topic of significant interest and discussion. Tjiptoherijanto's study in 2001 sheds light on the importance of the workforce's growth as a crucial determinant of economic growth, along with education and health levels.

The workforce, composed of individuals actively participating in the labor market, plays a pivotal role in the production process and overall economic performance of a country. As Tjiptoherijanto suggests, when the population increases, there is a simultaneous rise in the number of potential workers available. This expansion in the workforce provides an opportunity for countries to enhance their production capacity and subsequently achieve economic growth. With a larger pool of labor, more resources and skills can be employed in various sectors, leading to increased output and productivity.

Also, the link between population expansion and economic advancement is not a novel idea. In his 2006 book, Todaro highlights the historical importance of population increase and employment creation as drivers of successful economic results. The demand for products and services rises as the population grows, which can boost business activity and propel growth. Also, a larger consumer base that fosters domestic demand and offers a foundation for economic growth might result from an increase in the workforce.

The quality and skills of the labor force are equally important, despite the fact that population increase and an enlarged workforce may have the potential to contribute to economic growth. The levels of education and health are crucial components in determining a nation's human capital. By making financial investments in healthcare and education, people may develop the talents, knowledge, and skills required to make meaningful contributions to the economy. An educated and healthy workforce is more likely to engage in innovative and entrepreneurial activities, which are important factors in driving economic growth.

Overall, Tjiptoherijanto's study, supported by Todaro's perspective, highlights the interconnectedness of population growth, workforce expansion, education levels, and economic development. By recognizing the significance of these factors and implementing policies that promote education, health, and job creation, countries can harness the potential of their workforce and propel sustainable economic growth. This understanding underscores the importance of considering population dynamics and human capital in shaping economic policies and strategies for long-term prosperity.

The link between population growth and economic growth can be observed through several mechanisms. As the population expands, there is a greater demand for goods and services, leading to an increase in job opportunities. The growing workforce not only creates a larger consumer base but also contributes to the overall economic activity within the domestic market. This dynamic relationship between population growth and job creation fosters a cycle of demand and supply, which further stimulates economic growth.

Moreover, population growth serves as an indicator of the health of the domestic economy. A larger market size is a result of a growing population, providing potential opportunities for businesses to cater to the demands and preferences of an expanding customer base. This progress in the domestic economy can lead to increased investments, entrepreneurship, and technological advancements, all of which contribute to additional economic expansion.

In light of the findings from the study conducted in West Java Province from 2017 to 2019, the significance of labor force variables, particularly the number of individuals with Diplomas or Bachelor's degrees, in driving economic development becomes evident. The estimated results reveal a substantial and positive impact on the overall progress of the region's economy. These findings align with established theories that emphasize the importance of a skilled and educated workforce for economic growth.

The study's findings also support the conclusions drawn in previous research, such as Eliza's (2015) study, which highlighted the statistical significance of the workforce in influencing economic growth. Eliza's research provided empirical evidence supporting the positive relationship between education levels and economic development. The convergence of these findings with the current study's results strengthens the validity and reliability of the conclusions drawn.

By corroborating existing theories and previous research in this field, the current study contributes to the broader understanding of the relationship between labor force variables and economic development. It provides empirical evidence that supports the notion that a well-educated workforce, represented by individuals with Diplomas or Bachelor's degrees, plays a crucial role in fostering economic growth. In summary, the estimated findings of the study reinforce existing theories and previous research conducted in the field, providing empirical evidence of the significant and beneficial impact of labor force variables, specifically the number of graduates with a Diploma or Bachelor's degree, on West Java's economic development. These findings emphasize the importance of investing in education and human capital development to drive sustainable economic growth in the region.

3.4 Most Dominant Variable Influence on Economic Growth

Based on the calculations conducted in this study, it has been determined that the education variable plays a pivotal role in influencing economic growth. The analysis reveals that the education variable possesses the highest coefficient value of 0.913 among all the variables considered, indicating its significant impact on economic development. This finding underscores the importance of education as a key factor in enhancing the quality of human resources.

The dominance of the education variable can be attributed to its multifaceted benefits. Education equips individuals with valuable knowledge, skills, and competencies that are essential for their personal and professional growth. By acquiring education, individuals are able to improve their cognitive abilities, critical thinking skills, and problem-solving capabilities. These enhanced capabilities subsequently contribute to increased productivity and efficiency in various sectors of the economy.

Furthermore, education promotes technical progress and creativity. Those with a higher level of education are more likely to engage in research and development activities, which leads to the production and adoption of new technologies. Technological breakthroughs propel economic growth by increasing productivity, establishing new sectors, and offering new job possibilities. Education is also important in aiding the transmission of knowledge and technology across industries, hence promoting overall economic development.

Education may be considered as a development investment with significant long-term rewards. It gives people more power, increases their employability, and allows them to contribute more effectively to the economy. Additionally, educated people are more likely to participate in creative activities, entrepreneurship, and knowledge-based sectors, all of which are important drivers of economic growth and prosperity.

The findings of this study align with global development goals and international agendas. The United Nations' Sustainable Development Goal 4 emphasizes the importance of quality education for inclusive and sustainable economic growth. By investing in education, regions can address various challenges, such as poverty, inequality, and unemployment, and lay the foundation for long-term economic development.

The findings of this study affirm that the education variable exerts the most significant influence on economic development. The positive impact of education on the quality of human resources, productivity, and long-term economic benefits highlights the critical role of education in fostering sustainable economic growth. By prioritizing education and investing in the development of a skilled and knowledgeable workforce, regions can unlock their potential and pave the way for a prosperous future. Education serves as a catalyst for economic progress, social inclusion, and overall well-being, making it an indispensable component of thriving societies.

IV. CONCLUSION

The study's conclusions support the notion that West Java Province's economy benefits from its population, health, and education levels. The degree of education among these variables stands out as the most important driver of regional economic growth. Investment in education is essential for promoting economic growth and should include initiatives to promote educational quality, provide fair access to school, and improve educational infrastructure.

In West Java Province, human capital's potential is crucially unlocked by education. Education promotes greater productivity, innovation, and general economic growth by providing people with the information, skills, and competences they need. It enables people to actively participate in the work force and take part in productive activities that promote economic growth.

In addition to education, the level of health and the size of the population also influence the region's economy. A healthy population contributes to higher productivity and labor force participation, leading to increased economic output. Moreover, a larger population creates a larger consumer market, attracting investments and stimulating economic activity. When combined with an educated workforce, these factors create a favorable environment for sustainable economic development in West Java Province.

However, it is crucial to acknowledge the limitations of the available data for measuring human capital accurately. The current statistics may not capture the full breadth of human capital in the region. Therefore, future research should focus on obtaining more comprehensive and representative data to provide a more accurate assessment of the region's human resources. By addressing this data limitation, policymakers and stakeholders can make informed decisions and develop effective strategies to support regional economic growth and development.

The analysis highlights the significant influence of education, health, and population on the economy of West Java Province. Education stands out as the most crucial determinant of economic development, followed by health and population. However, it is imperative to address the limitations of the available data in measuring human capital accurately. Future research should strive to obtain more representative data to enhance the understanding of the dynamics of human capital in the region. By doing so, policymakers and stakeholders can develop targeted interventions and policies to unlock the full potential of the region's human resources and promote sustainable economic growth in West Java Province.

REFERENCES

Amann, E., Aslanidis, N., Nixson, F., & Walters, B. (2006). "Economic Growth And Poverty Alleviation: A reconsideration of Dollar and Kraay." The European Journal of Development Research, 18(1), 22-44.

Asiedu, E. (2014). "Does Foreign Aid in Education Promote Economic Growth? Evidence from Sub-Saharan Africa." Journal of African Development, 16(1), 37-59.

Becker, G. S. (2009). "Human Capital: A Theoretical and Empirical Analysis, with Special Reference to Education." University of Chicago Press.

Camacho, M., Perez-Quiros, G., & Poncela, P. (2015). "Extracting Nonlinear Signals from Several Economic Indicators." Journal of Applied Econometrics, 30(7), 1073-1089.

Dwi-Atmanti, H. (2005). "Investasi Sumber Daya Manusia Melalui Pendidikan." Jurnal Dinamika Pembangunan (JDP), 2(Nomor 1), 30-39.

Eliza, Y. (2015). "Pengaruh Investasi, Angkatan Kerja dan Pengeluaran Pemerintah terhadap Pertumbuhan Ekonomi di Sumatera Barat." PEKBIS (Jurnal Pendidikan Ekonomi Dan Bisnis), 7(3), 198-208.

Fleisher, B., Li, H., & Zhao, M. Q. (2010). "Human Capital, Economic Growth, and Regional Inequality in China." Journal of Development Economics, 92(2), 215-231.

Handayani, N. S., Bendesa, I., & Yuliarmi, N. (2016). "Pengaruh Jumlah Penduduk, Angka Harapan Hidup, Rata-Rata Lama Sekolah, dan PDRB Per Kapita Terhadap Pertumbuhan Ekonomi di Provinsi Bali." Jurnal Ekonomi dan Bisnis Universitas Udayana, 5(10), 3449-3474.

Hanushek, E. A. (2013). "Economic Growth in Developing Countries: The Role of Human Capital." Economics of Education Review, 37, 204-212.

Kumar, C. S. (2006). "Human Capital and Growth Empirics." The Journal of Developing Areas, 153-179.

Martono, N. (2010). "Metode Penelitian Kuantitatif: Analisis Isi dan Analisis Data Sekunder." RajaGrafindo Persada.

Putri, R. F. (2015). "Analisis Pengaruh Inflasi, Pertumbuhan Ekonomi dan Upah Terhadap Pengangguran Terdidik." Economics Development Analysis Journal, 4(2), 175-181.

Solow, R. M. (1956). "A Contribution to the Theory of Economic Growth." The Quarterly Journal of Economics, 70(1), 65-94.

Spengler, J. J. (1977). "Adam Smith on Human Capital." The American Economic Review, 67(1), 32-36.

Sugiyono. (2011). "Metode Penelitian Kuantitatif, Kualitatif dan R&D." Bandung: Afabeta.

Suhendra, I., & Wicaksono, B. H. (2020). "Tingkat Pendidikan, Upah, Inflasi, dan Pertumbuhan Ekonomi Terhadap Pengangguran di Indonesia." Jurnal Ekonomi-Qu, 6(1).

Tjiptoherijanto, P. (2001). "Proyeksi Penduduk, Angkatan Kerja, Tenaga Kerja, dan Peran Serikat Pekerja dalam Peningkatan Kesejahteraan." Majalah Perencanaan Pembangunan, 23, 1-10.

Todaro, M. P., & Smith, S. C. (2006). "Pembangunan Ekonomi Jilid 1 Edisi Kesembilan." Jakarta: Erlangga.

Umiyati, E. (2014). "Analisa Pertumbuhan Ekonomi Dan Ketimpangan Pembangunan Antar Wilayah di Pulau Sumatera." Jurnal Paradigma Ekonomika, 9(2).

Woodhall, M. (1987). "Human Capital Concepts." Economics of Education (pp. 21-24).

Wujarso, R. (2021). The Influence of Human Capital on Economic Growth. International Journal of Science and Society, 3(2), 24-30.

About The Author

Riyanto Wujarso holds a Master of Management degree from Gadjah Mada University, Yogyakarta, Indonesia. With a strong background in economics and management, Riyanto is passionate about exploring the relationship between human capital and economic growth.

As an accomplished researcher and academic, Riyanto has dedicated his career to studying the impact of human capital on various aspects of the economy. His expertise lies in analyzing the role of human capital in driving economic growth, productivity, and competitiveness.

Currently, Riyanto is working on his upcoming book titled "The Influence of Human Capital on Economic Growth." This book aims to provide a comprehensive analysis of the relationship between human capital and economic development, exploring how investments in education, skills, and training contribute to sustainable economic growth.

Riyanto's research is backed by extensive literature review, empirical evidence, and statistical analysis, ensuring the book's content is grounded in solid academic research. Through this publication, Riyanto aims to contribute to the existing body of knowledge on the importance of human capital for economic progress and provide valuable insights for policymakers, economists, and scholars.

In addition to his research pursuits, Riyanto is also actively involved in teaching and mentoring students in the field of economics and management. His dedication to academic excellence and passion for promoting sustainable economic growth make him a respected figure in his field.

Riyanto's commitment to advancing knowledge and understanding in the realm of human capital and economic growth is evident through his research endeavors and the forthcoming book. With his expertise and contributions, Riyanto aims to shape discussions and policies related to human capital development and its implications for economic prosperity.